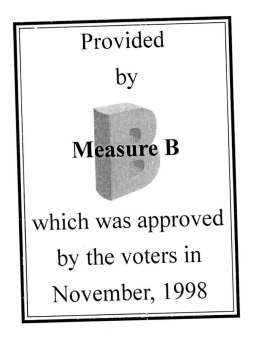

Provided

by

**Measure B**

which was approved

by the voters in

November, 1998

ULYSSES S. GRANT.

# ENCYCLOPEDIA
# of PRESIDENTS

---

# *Ulysses S. Grant*

*Eighteenth President of the United States*

By Zachary Kent

*Consultant: Charles Abele, Ph.D.*
*Social Studies Instructor*
*Chicago Public School System*

CHILDRENS PRESS ®

CHICAGO

**Grant with his wife, children, and grandchildren**

**Library of Congress Cataloging-in-Publication Data**

Kent, Zachary.
    Ulysses S. Grant / by Zachary Kent.
        p.        cm. — (Encyclopedia of presidents)
    Includes index.
    Summary: Follows the military and political career of the
general who became the "Hero of Appomattox" and the
eighteenth president of the United States.
    ISBN 0-516-01364-5
    1.    Grant, Ulysses S. (Ulysses Simpson), 1822-1885 — Juvenile
literature.    2.    Presidents — United States — Biography —
Juvenile literature.    3.    Generals — United States — Biography —
Juvenile literature.    4.    United States. Army — Biography —
Juvenile literature.    5.    United States — History — Civil War,
1861-1865 — Campaigns — Juvenile literature.    6.    United
States — Politics and government — 1869-1877 — Juvenile
literature.    [1.    Grant, Ulysses S. (Ulysses Simpson), 1822-
1885.    2.    Presidents.]    I.    Title.    II.    Series.
E672.K46    1989
973.8'2'0924 — dc19                                              88-38056
[B]                                                                        CIP
[92]                                                                      AC

**Picture Acknowledgments**

AP/Wide World Photos — 26, 34, 50, 53, 56, 57,
69, 73 (top right), 76, 80 (2 pictures)

The Bettmann Archive, Inc. — 4, 35, 36, 39, 54,
61, 62, 75

Historical Pictures Service, Chicago — 5, 6, 9, 11,
12, 15 (2 pictures), 19, 22, 27, 30, 32, 33, 43,
46, 47, 51, 52, 58, 59 (2 pictures), 60, 72, 73
(top left and bottom), 74, 82, 85 (2 pictures), 87,
89

Library of Congress — 25, 38, 42, 65, 67, 70, 78

North Wind Picture Archives — 40

Special Collections Division, U.S. Military
Academy Library — 16, 17, 18

U.S. Bureau of Printing and Engraving — 2

Cover design and illustration
by Steven Gaston Dobson

    14 15 16 17 18 19 20 R 02 01 00

Grant's tomb on Riverside Drive in New York City

# Table of Contents

# Chapter 1

# The Fighting General

Thousands of blue-clad Union soldiers crouched in wide-eyed panic and hugged the muddy riverbank. Less than three miles away a terrific battle raged. Cannon thundered and cracking muskets sent bullets whistling through the air. At dawn on Sunday, April 6, 1862, 40,000 Confederate troops had launched a surprise attack against the 42,000-man Union army encamped at Pittsburg Landing, Tennessee. As the screaming rebels smashed through the Union picket line, many startled Yankees abandoned their tents and campfires. They retreated through the woods, running all the way to the Tennessee River.

At 8:00 A.M. a steamboat hurriedly arrived at the river landing. On deck stood Major General Ulysses S. Grant, commander of the Union troops. Riding his horse ashore, the bearded thirty-nine-year-old general saw the hordes of frightened soldiers hiding under cover of the river bluff. Grimly determined to save his army, Grant immediately began issuing instructions to his staff officers. First he arranged to have more ammunition sent to the men still fighting at the front. Then he ordered distant generals to speed along badly needed reinforcements. That done, he spurred his horse forward into the thick of the battle.

Opposite page: General Grant's arrival
on the battlefield of Shiloh, Tennessee

Along the battlefront the fighting roared in savage confusion. In thick woods and dense underbrush Union regiments fiercely struggled to hold their ground. In a peach orchard, rebel bullets tore through the blossoms until the petals rained down like confetti. Nearby, desperate for drinks of water, wounded soldiers crawled to a pond. By day's end, it was renamed "Bloody Pond." Farther away, cannon shells screamed through the air near a crude log church called the Shiloh Meeting House.

Smoking a cigar, General Grant calmly trotted among his troops and observed the situation. "During the whole of Sunday," he explained, "I was continuously engaged in passing from one part of the field to another, giving directions to division commanders."

Near the Shiloh church, Grant encountered General William Tecumseh Sherman. Sherman remained fearless and believed his division could hold on if given more shells and cartridges. Grant promised him the ammunition and then cantered off to see General Benjamin Prentiss at the center of the Union line. Crouched along a sunken road, the men of Prentiss's division were stoutly resisting all enemy attacks. Grant commanded Prentiss to hold his position at all cost. Soon bullets flew so thickly along the road that it became known as the "Hornet's Nest."

Everywhere Grant appeared, he inspired his troops to renewed effort. The sight of their general riding calmly about filled the men with hope that all was not lost. Often he exposed himself where the danger was greatest. At one small clearing, bullets whizzed about Grant and his staff until one nervous officer pleaded, "General, we must

**Grant commanding his troops at the Battle of Shiloh**

leave this place. It isn't necessary to stay here. If we do we shall all be dead in five minutes." Coolly Grant gazed about and finally muttered, "I guess that's so."

Throughout the afternoon the bloody fight continued. Relentlessly the gray-clad Confederates attacked. As the numbers of killed and wounded increased, many shaken Union regiments fell back toward the river. In the Hornet's Nest General Prentiss's division discovered itself completely surrounded, and late in the afternoon Prentiss surrendered his remaining 2,200 men.

9

As the sun set, the Union army appeared on the verge of total defeat. It had been a very bad day for the Yankees. The ground around the Shiloh church lay littered with the dead and dying. Shocked soldiers wandered away through the woods or cowered along the riverbank. That night a cold rain fell as artillery shells crashed among the trees. Colonel James McPherson discovered Grant standing beside a smoldering fire. McPherson reported that one-third of the army was destroyed and all the rest of the men were disheartened. "General Grant, under this condition of affairs," he questioned, "what do you propose to do, sir? Shall I make preparations for retreat?"

Quickly Grant responded, "Retreat? No. I propose to attack at daylight and whip them."

Grant's tough attitude greatly impressed his men. Through the stormy night, broken regiments reformed themselves. Fresh brigades ferried across the river while others marched in from the north along a country road. At dawn Grant renewed the fighting. The Confederate army after the fight of the previous day was weak and tired. Its commanding general, Albert Sidney Johnston, lay dead, and it had no reinforcements to draw upon. Union infantrymen cheered themselves hoarse when they discovered the rebels retreating.

The Union army had hung on. By refusing to quit, they had won the Battle of Shiloh, the bloodiest battle ever fought in America up to that time. The 17,000 Union and Confederate casualties of the two-day battle stunned the people of the North. Many complained that Grant had been drunk when the battle started and should not have been

Pittsburg Landing, Tennessee, a few days after the battle

surprised. Others claimed he should have retreated and saved his men from needless bloodshed. Grant made no apologies. He understood the brutal fact that only hard fighting won wars. Before the conflict ended, he predicted, the "country will have to mourn the loss of many brave men." President Abraham Lincoln agreed. "I can't spare this man," he told Grant's critics. "He fights."

The outbreak of the American Civil War in 1861 had found Ulysses S. Grant working as a simple clerk in his father's Galena, Illinois, leather goods store. By 1865, however, Grant's stubborn courage and unyielding spirit would make him a national military hero. Grant's victories helped defeat the Confederate armies and reunite the North and South. Grateful Americans would reward the popular warrior in 1868 by electing him eighteenth president of the United States.

# Chapter 2

# Jesse Grant's Pride and Joy

The waters of the great Ohio River swirled past a wooded bluff at Point Pleasant, Ohio. Inside a little two-room cabin that stood nearby, Hiram Ulysses Grant was born on April 27, 1822. A gathering of relatives chose the baby's name. His parents preferred to call him by his middle name, Ulysses, the name of the ancient Greek warrior who had helped win the siege of Troy.

Ulysses's mother, Hannah Simpson Grant, possessed the traits of a strong willed but silent farm woman. "I never saw my mother cry," declared Ulysses in later years. Neighbors knew his father, Jesse Root Grant, as a hard-working tanner who cured leather from the hides of animals. A talkative man, Jesse Grant enjoyed arguing about politics. Though five other boys and girls would follow, Jesse let people know he was especially proud of his first child. "My Ulysses," he exclaimed, was "a most beautiful child."

In 1823 Jesse Grant carted his wife and baby son twenty-five miles to Georgetown, Ohio. In that new community he expected a great demand for leather boots and harnesses. On a parcel of farmland he constructed a small brick house, and across the street he built his tannery.

Ulysses showed a love for horses at a very early age. "Who will ride the pony?" asked the ringmaster of a traveling circus that one day visited town. Two-year-old Ulysses begged for a chance, and held upon the trained pony's back he gleefully rounded the ring several times. During the next years the little boy often played in the straw among the horses in his father's stable. Neighbors sometimes watched in horror as the child crawled between the mighty hooves of strange horse teams stopping at the tannery. Unworried, his mother quietly commented, "Horses seem to understand Ulysses." By the age of five the boy could stand upon a trotting horse's back, balancing himself with the reins.

Ulysses hated the work at his father's growing tannery. The bloody animal skins and smelly vats of curing chemicals made him sick to his stomach. But the boy found other ways to help the family.

"When I was seven or eight years of age," he remembered, "I began hauling all the wood used in the house and shops. . . . When about eleven years old, I was strong enough to hold a plough. From that age until seventeen I did all the work done with horses, such as breaking up the land, furrowing, ploughing corn and potatoes [and] bringing in the crops when harvested. . . ." Ulysses's mastery with horses sometimes earned him money when neighbors brought him untamed horses to break and train. He also ran a travel service, carrying passengers by wagon to distant towns and back. For pleasure the young man recalled "going to the creek a mile away to swim in summer [or] . . . skating on the ice in winter. . . ."

Hannah Simpson Grant                    Jesse Root Grant

Ulysses began attending Georgetown's subscription school when he was five. In the little one-room schoolhouse, boys and girls of all ages crowded onto wooden benches and learned "the three R's, Reading, 'Riting, 'Rithmetic." As he grew older Ulysses showed a special skill at solving arithmetic problems in his head. At home his parents never felt a need to punish him. Classmates later recalled that he also behaved well in school.

In truth, Ulysses was quite a bashful young man. One Georgetown girl later remarked, "he was a real nice boy who never had anything to say and when he said anything, he always said it short." Classmate Jimmy Sanderson noted that he "always seemed to be thinking, and to take things that excited us—so easy. I don't remember that I ever saw him excited." A lot of people in Georgetown misunderstood Ulysses's awkward shyness. They thought him dull and stupid. Sometimes smart alecks mispronounced his name and called him "Useless" Grant.

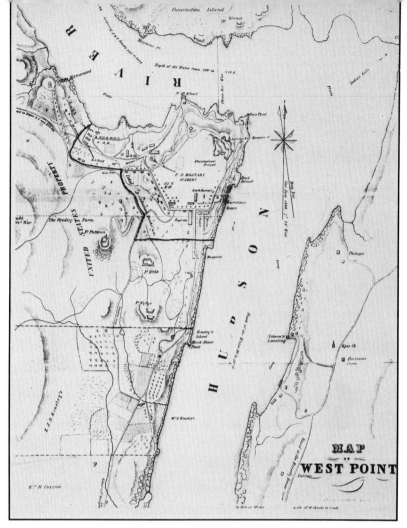

The U.S. Military Academy at West Point, on the Hudson River

While sixteen-year-old Ulysses attended a winter term at the Presbyterian Academy at Ripley, Ohio, in 1838, Jesse figured out an inexpensive way to advance his son's learning. The United States Military Academy at West Point, New York, provided cadets with a fine education, and the U.S. government paid all the expenses. Quickly Jesse Grant applied to his old friend Congressman Thomas L. Hamer for an appointment for Ulysses. Ulysses first learned of his father's plan during his Christmas visit home from Ripley.

**A view of West Point from nearby Fort Putnam**

"Ulysses," his father stated, "I believe you are going to receive the appointment."

"What appointment?" asked the surprised teenager.

"To West Point. I have applied for it."

"But I won't go!" Ulysses protested.

Flinty old Jesse Grant, however, had already made up his mind. As Ulysses later recalled the scene, "He said he thought I would, *and I thought so too, if he did.*"

**Officers on the West Point grounds in 1841**

In the end Ulysses reluctantly agreed to attend West Point, although he revealed, "A military life had no charms for me. . . ." Traveling east, Grant arrived at West Point on May 29, 1839. The young Ohioan climbed up the hill from the Hudson River steamboat landing and soon presented himself at the adjutant's office. There the boy discovered that Congressman Hamer had mistakenly registered his name as Ulysses Simpson Grant. His first name, Hiram, was gone and his mother's maiden name, Simpson, had been inserted instead. Grant wished to avoid being teased about his initials H. U. G., so he accepted the change without too much argument. His classmates, however, soon joked about his new name, U. S. Grant. "United States Grant," they called him. "Uncle Sam Grant!" Before long the nickname "Uncle Sam" stuck, and then they simply shortened it to "Sam."

West Point cadet uniforms
in 1840 (left to right):
winter field uniform,
full dress uniform,
and field uniform

"A more unpromising boy never entered the Military Academy," remembered Senior Cadet William Tecumseh Sherman. Small in size and boyish in appearance, Cadet Grant quickly learned the academy routine. Drum rolls shook him awake each dawn. He marched, drilled, and stood at attention for roll calls and inspections. At every moment, instructors and upperclassmen passed judgment on his skills, appearance, and habits. "I came near forgetting to tell you about our demerit or 'black marks,'" Grant wrote to a cousin. "They give a man one of these 'black marks' for almost nothing, and if he gets two hundred a year they dismiss him." For talking in ranks, sloppy dress, and other misbehavior, Grant received ninety-eight demerits during his junior year.

Grant also failed to take his schoolwork very seriously. He often preferred reading romantic novels. "In his studies he was lazy and careless," one of his roommates, Rufus Ingalls, remembered. "Instead of studying a lesson, he would merely read it over once or twice."

It was as a horseman that Grant made his greatest impression at West Point. Cadet James Longstreet declared he was "the most daring horseman in the Academy." One day Grant set an Academy high jump record that lasted for twenty-five years.

As the finest horseman in the graduating class of 1843, Grant hoped for an assignment in the cavalry. But because of his rank in class (21 in a class of 39), he did not get his choice. Instead, as a new second lieutenant in the U.S. Army, Grant received orders to join the Fourth Infantry Regiment stationed in Saint Louis, Missouri.

Grant bade farewell to West Point and journeyed westward. "On the 30th of September [1843] I reported for duty at Jefferson Barracks, St. Louis," he later recalled. At the age of twenty-one he stood five feet seven inches tall. His uniform fit snugly on his small, slender frame. Because of Grant's rosy skin and soft features, his fellow officers often called him "The Little Beauty."

The family of Lieutenant Grant's senior class roommate, Fred Dent, owned a plantation called White Haven just five miles away. One day Grant rode out to pay his respects. The Dent family welcomed him and soon he made regular visits. "He's as pretty as a doll," exclaimed eight-year-old Emmy Dent when she first saw the handsome soldier. Later she remembered that his hair was "fine and brown, very thick and wavy; his eyes were a clear blue and full of light."

It was Emmy's seventeen-year-old sister, Julia, who gradually captured Grant's attention. Although an eye problem caused her to squint, Julia had a lively personality and was an expert horsewoman. Often little Emmy Dent watched the two gallop off for "many a fine ride before breakfast or through the sunset and twilight after supper." Before many months Grant had fallen in love.

In the spring of 1844 trouble brewed between the United States and Mexico. Just beyond the Sabine River in Louisiana lay the Republic of Texas. Hard-fought battles such as those at the Alamo and San Jacinto had won American settlers in Texas their independence from Mexico in 1836. Texans had wished to join the United States then, but the slavery question presented many problems. In 1844, when negotiations to annex Texas finally began, the embittered Mexicans threatened war.

On May 7 the U.S. War Department ordered the Fourth Infantry to Fort Jesup in southwestern Louisiana. The troops gathering there were to act as a "corps of observation." Before he left, Grant hurried out to the Dents' home in White Haven for a final visit. During a buggy ride with Julia the lieutenant found a chance to speak his heart. Julia seemed fearful as they crossed a bridge flooded over with water. "I'm going to cling to you no matter what happens," she exclaimed, grasping his arm. After they safely reached the other side Grant turned to her and asked, "How would you like to cling to me for the rest of your life?" Happily Julia consented to become his wife.

# Chapter 3

# Years of Glory

Lieutenant Grant's military duty called him south before he and Julia could be married. For the next year the Fourth Infantry, as well as other regiments commanded by General Zachary Taylor, remained encamped in Louisiana. In spring 1845 Secretary of State James Buchanan instructed Taylor to move his army closer to the Mexican border of Texas, just annexed in March. "Texas must be protected from hostile invasion," Buchanan insisted.

Overland and by boat, the army traveled to the village of Corpus Christi, Texas. In this flat country of thorny cactus and thick chaparral, four thousand troops—half the entire U.S. Army—pitched tents and built fires. While the army awaited further orders, Lieutenant Grant netted turtles and oysters, broke wild horses, and otherwise made himself useful about camp.

On December 29, 1845, Texas officially joined the Union. Many soldiers greeted this news with cheers and celebrations. Grant, however, realized that war with Mexico loomed closer than ever. The United States claimed the Rio Grande as Texas's boundary, but Mexico disagreed. In March 1846 Grant's regiment marched 180 miles south to the Rio Grande.

Opposite page: Grant as a lieutenant
in the Mexican War in 1846

Taylor's "Army of Occupation" soon encamped beside the waters of the Rio Grande across from the Mexican town of Matamoros. On April 25, 1846, the smoldering powder keg of war finally exploded. Mexican soldiers ambushed and slaughtered an American scouting party on the north side of the river. "Hostilities," Taylor informed President James K. Polk, "may be considered as commenced."

Grant soon tasted battle for the first time. After marching most of his army to the coast to collect supplies, General Taylor started back to Fort Brown, a stockade he had built opposite Matamoros. As the soldiers loaded wagons, cannonfire suddenly roared in the distance. Fort Brown was under attack. Grant nervously listened to the thundering noise and afterwards admitted, "I felt sorry that I had enlisted."

Determined to rescue the besieged fort, General Taylor ordered his two thousand men onward. On May 8, 1846, the Americans encountered a large Mexican army blocking the road in front of them. Dotted with muddy waterholes and backed by a thicket of tall trees, the place was called Palo Alto.

Quickly General Taylor formed his troops for battle. Artillery batteries hurried forward to duel with the cannon of the enemy. Grant watched as exploding shells and cannonballs shrieked through the air. "One cannon-ball passed through our ranks, not far from me," exclaimed Grant. "It took off the head of an enlisted man and the underjaw of Captain Page of my regiment. . . ." Still Grant kept his position. "I scarcely thought of the . . . possibility of being touched myself, although nine-pound shots were

The Americans fight to victory in the Battle of Palo Alto.

whistling all around." The battle raged throughout the afternoon. As the sun set on the smoky battlefield, the weakened Mexicans withdrew. The Americans had scored a victory at Palo Alto.

On the following day the Americans continued their march toward Fort Brown. "When we advanced about six miles," Grant recalled, "we found that the enemy had taken up a new position in the midst of a dense woods." General Taylor charged his troops ahead and drove the enemy from this place called Resaca de la Palma. "Grape shot and musket balls were let fly from both sides making dreadful havoc," remembered Grant. "Our men continued to advance . . . in spite of the shots. . . . The Mexicans fought hard for an hour and a half but . . . finally commenced to retreat helter-skelter."

The siege of Monterrey

"Our victory has been decisive," reported General Taylor, and " . . . the causes . . . are doubtless to be found in the superior quality of our officers and men." Within days the beaten Mexicans abandoned Matamoros. Grant and his fellow soldiers soon welcomed thousands of fresh American troops into the conquered town. These volunteers had hurried southward as soon as Congress formally had declared war on Mexico.

General Taylor next marched his army toward the Mexican city of Monterrey. In the summer of 1846, Taylor's army of 6,600 soldiers broke camp and headed into Mexico's Sierra Madre Mountains. The Fourth Infantry Regiment needed a quartermaster to handle the transportation by mule trains of its food supplies and baggage. Because of

Grant making a run for ammunition through the streets of Monterrey

his well-known skill with four-legged animals, Lieutenant Grant received the thankless task. Each morning the troops marched off, leaving Grant and his men to clean up.

"After they had started, the tents and cooking utensils had to be made into packages, so that they could be lashed to the backs of the mules," remembered Grant. Sometimes mules resisted being loaded down, braying and kicking until their packs broke free and scattered across the ground. In spite of delays, Grant often surprised his comrades by the end of each day. Lieutenant Alexander Hays later marveled, "There was no road . . . so obstructed . . . but that Grant, in some mysterious way, would work his train through and have it in the camp of his brigade before the campfires were lighted."

By September 21 the American army reached Monterrey. Its many forts and the thick stone walls of its houses made it a powerful Mexican position. Fearlessly General Taylor split his army and ordered attacks into Monterrey from the east and west. As regimental quartermaster, Grant's duty was at the rear. At the first sound of gunfire, however, he later recalled, "I mounted a horse and rode to the front to see what was going on. I had been there but a short time when an order to charge was given, and lacking the moral courage to return to camp—where I had been ordered to stay—I charged with the regiment."

Two days later the furious battle resumed and again Grant showed his bravery. Inching forward street by street, General John Garland suddenly realized his soldiers needed more ammunition. Grant volunteered to carry the important message. Hanging onto the side of his horse he galloped off. "It was only at street crossings that my horse was under fire," he later revealed, "but these I crossed at such a flying rate that generally I was past and under cover of the next block of houses before the enemy fired. I got out safely without a scratch."

Another day of violent fighting and the Americans neared Monterrey's central square. Losing hope, the Mexicans agreed to surrender the city and march away. Three times Zachary Taylor had beaten his Mexican opponents against great odds. In the streets of Monterrey American troops loudly cheered the tough soldier they called "Old Rough and Ready." Taylor's fighting style especially impressed Lieutenant Grant. "General Taylor never wore uniform, but dressed himself entirely for comfort," he remembered. During battle, instead of remaining safely at the rear, "he moved about the field . . . to see through his own eyes the situation."

Ordered to join a new army being formed by General Winfield Scott in January 1847, many veteran soldiers were sorry to say goodbye to General Taylor. But the War Department had agreed to a daring plan proposed by General Scott. He intended to land at Vera Cruz on the Gulf of Mexico coast, march deep into the heart of the country, and capture Mexico City.

After sailing down the coast, Scott's army of 10,000 men came ashore on March 9. Within days Vera Cruz surrendered and Scott began his inland march. Along the mountain roads leading to Mexico City, the Americans pushed ahead. At Cerro Gordo and Churubusco they forced defending Mexicans to retreat. By September they had reached the outskirts of the Mexican capital.

In heavy fighting the dauntless American army forced its way into the city. Through the smoke and gunfire Grant as usual took an active role. Near the Mexican garrison at San Cosme, Grant and a few others hauled a small cannon up the steps of a church tower. "The shots from our little gun," Grant remarked, "dropped in upon the enemy and created great confusion." By day's end, all of Mexico City fell. On September 14, 1847, the U.S. Army proudly paraded into the city's central plaza while bands blared "Yankee Doodle." General Scott had proven that an army could thrust 260 miles into hostile territory with success, and Grant would never forget the lesson. The capture of Mexico City effectively ended the Mexican War.

Galena, Illinois, home of Ulysses and Julia Grant

# Chapter 4

# Years of Failure

For his brave and faithful service, Grant received a promotion to first lieutenant. While peace negotiations progressed, Grant operated a bakery to feed his regiment and on horseback he explored the Mexican countryside. "Everything looks as if peace should be established soon," he wrote Julia, "but perhaps my anxiety to get back to see again my Dearest Julia makes me argue this." Finally, in March 1848, the Senate ratified the Treaty of Guadalupe Hidalgo. In exchange for $15,000,000, the defeated Mexicans gave the United States all of the land north of the Rio Grande. This included both the New Mexico and the California territories.

As soon as possible Grant traveled north to Saint Louis. After four long years of engagement, twenty-six-year-old Ulysses S. Grant and twenty-two-year-old Julia Dent exchanged marriage vows at her parents' Saint Louis home on August 22, 1848. It was "a sweet, old-fashioned wedding," as young Emmy Dent remembered it.

The Dents' Saint Louis home, where Ulysses and Julia were married

During the next four years the newlyweds lived at border outposts at Detroit, Michigan, and Sackets Harbor, New York. When not performing his duties as regimental quartermaster, Grant enjoyed racing horses. Most often, however, he preferred to stay at home with his loving bride. On May 30, 1850, Grant proudly told neighbors of the birth of his first son, Frederick.

Grant's days of contentment ended in the spring of 1852. New orders arrived sending the Fourth Infantry west to the Pacific coast. Grant understood he must make the journey without Julia because she was expecting another child.

Instead of ordering an overland route across the Great Plains and the Rocky Mountains, the War Department had

San Francisco and its harbor in 1852

the regiment sail to Panama. (It would be years before the Panama Canal, connecting the Atlantic and the Pacific oceans, was built.) When the troops arrived, they hiked across the narrow isthmus and boarded other ships on the western coast. As he stumbled along the steaming jungle trail, Grant watched many soldiers drop and die. The dreaded disease cholera killed about one-third of the people who journeyed with his mule train.

In September 1852, the ship *Golden Gate* brought Grant into San Francisco harbor. The boom town bustled as prospectors still hurried to take part in the California Gold Rush. From San Francisco the Fourth Infantry steamed north to Fort Vancouver on the Columbia River in Oregon Territory.

**Julia Dent Grant, Ulysses's wife**

Life at this peaceful frontier outpost proved boring and frustrating for the thirty-year-old officer. Grant longed to have his wife and children with him. His second son, Ulysses, Jr., had been born by this time, but of course Grant had never seen him. He realized, too, that he could not support his family in the West on his $680 yearly army salary.

"He seemed to be always sad," one sergeant later remembered of Grant. In one letter to Julia, Grant mourned, "I . . . could enjoy myself here as well as at any place that I have ever been stationed if only you were here." More and more often the homesick lieutenant drank whiskey in an attempt to forget his loneliness. A promotion to captain and a transfer to Fort Humboldt in

**Troops marching through San Francisco in 1853**

northern California in 1853 failed to help. "I sometimes get so anxious to see you and our little boys, that I am almost tempted to resign," he soon wrote Julia.

In the end, Grant's continued drinking aroused the anger of Fort Humboldt's commander. When Colonel Robert Buchanan discovered Grant drunk in public one day in April 1854, he demanded that the captain either resign or stand trial. Promptly Grant wrote out his letter of resignation, ending fifteen years in the military. Gossip about Grant traveled quickly through the army. His reputation as a drunkard would haunt him for the rest of his life. But as he started east, full of optimism, he told his friends, "Whoever hears of me in ten years, will hear of a well-to-do old Missouri farmer."

Hardscrabble, the farmhouse Grant built near Saint Louis, Missouri

Reunited with his wife at last in the summer of 1854, Grant remarked, "I was now to commence at the age of thirty-two, a new struggle for our support." For one season Grant hoed potatoes on a farm owned by his brother-in-law. At the same time he cleared sixty acres of land near Saint Louis that Julia's father had given her. Cutting heavy timbers in 1856, Grant built a sturdy but plain farmhouse, which he named Hardscrabble.

Grant worked hard to make the farm a success. In the springtime he plowed the land and planted oats, corn, and wheat. Bad luck, however, seemed to follow after him. Freezing weather damaged his crops, and falling prices further cut his income. Grant soon depended on chopping and selling wood to feed his growing family. A daughter, Nellie, had been born in 1855 and a third son, Jesse, in 1858. Things got so bad that one Christmas Grant pawned his watch to buy gifts for his wife and children.

Sometimes old army friends encountered Grant selling wood on Saint Louis street corners. With his drooping shoulders and shaggy beard, only Grant's faded blue army overcoat reminded people that he once had been a soldier. "Grant, what are you doing," exclaimed a surprised officer one day. "I am solving the problem of poverty," quietly answered Grant.

After coughing and shaking with fever through much of 1858, Grant admitted his failure as a farmer. "In the fall of 1858," he sadly explained, "I sold out my stock, crops and farming utensils at auction, and gave up farming." Although troubled by debts, Grant kindly set free his only slave, William, a faithful field hand.

Harry Boggs, a cousin of Julia's, agreed to hire Grant at his Saint Louis real estate firm. Printed business cards soon advertised, "Boggs & Grant, General Agents, Collect Rents, Negociate Loans, Buy and Sell Real Estate, etc." As a real estate agent, Grant showed himself not aggressive enough to sell property and too kind to collect rents. Josiah McClellan, who shared the office space, observed, "He doesn't seem to be just calculated for business of that sort. But an honester, more generous man never lived. I don't believe that he knows what dishonesty is." Grant's year in the real estate business proved a complete failure too.

In the spring of 1860 Grant swallowed his pride and appealed to his father for work. Jesse Grant owned two tanneries now, as well as three leather goods stores. Although deeply disappointed with the many failures of his thirty-eight-year-old son, Jesse offered him a job clerking in his Galena, Illinois, store with an $800-a-year salary.

The Grants' residence in Galena, Illinois

A tooting steamboat whistle announced the arrival of the Grant family at Galena in the summer of 1860. A small brick house perched at 121 High Street served as their home. Each morning Grant stepped down the steep hill to the leather goods store on Main Street. Grant's younger brothers, Simpson and Orvil, actually ran the store, which sold bridles, harnesses, whips, and saddles. Visitors usually glimpsed Ulysses bent over a ledger in the back room, keeping the accounts. Sometimes, though, he unloaded wagons or waited upon customers. Galena citizen John E. Smith remembered, "Grant was a very poor businessman. . . . If a customer called . . . [Grant] would go behind the counter, very reluctantly, and drag down whatever was wanted; but hardly ever knew the price of it, and in nine cases out of ten, charged either too much or too little."

Grant chatting with friends in a Galena hardware store

People took no interest in the quiet ex-army captain. At the end of each workday he passed through the streets unnoticed. Now, having failed at every undertaking, he found his only comfort in his family. "Mister, do you want to fight?" three-year-old Jesse gleefully challenged his father when he arrived home each night. "I'm a man of peace," Grant always replied, "but I'll not be hectored by a person of your size." Then father and son would wrestle together and laugh.

Grant might have spent the remainder of his days as a leather goods clerk, bothered by memories of failure. National events, however, were fated to change his life. In November 1860, Americans elected Abraham Lincoln sixteenth president of the United States. Soon people in the North and South excitedly talked of civil war.

# Chapter 5

# "Unconditional Surrender"

"The South will fight," Ulysses S. Grant correctly guessed.

For over forty years, arguments over slavery had raged across the United States. The busy factories of the industrial North employed European immigrants. Northerners had no use for slavery, and many people considered it to be cruel and immoral. In the South, however, where cotton was the most important product, plantation owners greatly depended upon black slaves to plant and pick their crops.

The crisis finally erupted with the presidential election of Abraham Lincoln of Illinois. Angry southerners feared Lincoln planned to abolish slavery. Rather than submit, eleven southern states quit the Union. Together they formed the Confederate States of America, with Jefferson Davis as their president. Many of Grant's old southern army friends joined the Confederate army. In April 1861, Confederate cannoneers bombarded Fort Sumter in the Charleston, South Carolina, harbor.

Opposite page: General Grant in 1861

The Confederate attack on Fort Sumter, South Carolina, in 1861

On April 16, men rushed from the Galena telegraph office to spread the latest news. The Union garrison at Fort Sumter had surrendered. President Lincoln was calling for 75,000 loyal volunteers to put down the rebellion. With the outbreak of war, Grant reached a grim decision. "I thought I had done with soldiering," he commented. "I never expected to be in military life again. But . . . if my knowledge and experience can be of any service, I think I ought to offer them."

The only man in town with real army training, thirty-nine-year-old Grant drilled Galena's company of volunteers and marched with them to Springfield. The Illinois

Congressman John Logan rallies Illinoisans for the Union side.

state capital buzzed with excitement as thousands of volunteers arrived. For a while Grant worked as a clerk for the governor, helping to organize the state troops into regiments. In the meantime he wrote to the War Department hoping to receive a military commission. When he heard nothing, he next traveled to Cincinnati, Ohio, to see district commander General George McClellan. For two days Grant patiently sat in an outer office, but McClellan would not see him. He probably remembered Grant's bad reputation as a drinker.

Just as Grant unhappily prepared to return to Galena, he received a telegram from Illinois governor Richard Yates. It offered him command of the Twenty-First Illinois Volunteer Regiment with the rank of colonel. Many of the 600 volunteers in that regiment were known to be rowdy troublemakers. Still Grant gladly accepted the assignment. "They're an unruly lot. Do you think you can manage them?" someone asked him. "Oh, yes," Grant answered, "I can manage them." Under Grant's command, tough discipline and constant drill soon whipped even the wildest farmboys into obedient soldiers.

Colonel Grant's first engagement with the enemy occurred in northern Missouri in July 1861. As he marched his regiment toward the Confederate encampment of Colonel Thomas Harris, Grant later admitted, ". . . my heart kept getting higher and higher until it felt to me as though it was in my throat. I would have given anything then to have been back in Illinois, but . . . I kept right on. When we reached a point from which the valley below was in full view I halted."

With great surprise, he discovered the Confederate camp had been abandoned. "My heart resumed its place," he explained. "It occurred to me at once that Harris had been as much afraid of me as I had been of him. . . . From that event to the close of the war, I never experienced [fear] upon confronting an enemy. . . . The lesson was valuable."

Grant had proven himself a capable officer, and President Lincoln promoted him to brigadier general in August 1861. His new assignment sent him to the Cairo district in southern Illinois. The War Department hoped to recapture the Mississippi River and force the enemy out of Kentucky, Missouri, and Tennessee. Eagerly Grant prepared to take part in this plan.

With a force of 3,000 men, the general ferried across the Mississippi River on November 7, 1861. At Belmont, Missouri, the Union soldiers attacked a Confederate camp. Men shouted wildly and muskets loudly cracked. "Early in this engagement my horse was shot under me," declared Grant, "but I got another . . . and kept well up with the advance. . . ."

The Yankee troops overran the rebel camp, but soon the enemy brought up reinforcements. Some fearful Union officers yelled that they had been surrounded. Sternly Grant told them that "we had cut our way in and could cut our way out just as well. . . ."

Through woods and cornfields Grant hurried his men back to the river. Then he calmly waited on the riverbank while his troops reboarded their boats. As the Confederates approached, their commander remarked, "There is a Yankee; you may try your marksmanship on him if you wish." Remarkably, no one shot at Grant and he escaped with his life.

Grant regarded his raid on Belmont a success. His soldiers, he believed, had "acquired a confidence in themselves that did not desert them through the war." Grant's next plan of attack required the courage of just such veteran troops. With War Department approval Grant prepared to attack two Confederate strongholds, Fort Henry and Fort Donelson, in Tennessee.

Grant's troops overrun the Confederate camp at Belmont, Missouri.

With 17,000 men and U.S. Navy gunboats as escort, Grant steamed up the Tennessee River. A powerful naval bombardment forced the Confederates to abandon Fort Henry on February 6, 1862. These rebels retreated overland twelve miles to Fort Donelson, on the Cumberland River. Promptly Grant marched his army in pursuit and soon surrounded Fort Donelson.

On February 14 the roaring cannon of four Union gunboats traded fire with Confederate artillery inside the fort. Two of the gunboats soon limped downstream in crippled condition. The next day rebel troops charged out of the fort and smashed into the right side of the Union lines. The surprised bluecoats reeled back in panic.

Grant—known as the "muddiest man in the army"—at Fort Donelson

Arriving at that part of the field, Grant immediately understood the situation. To his shaken troops he shouted, "Fill your cartridge boxes quick, and get into line; the enemy is trying to escape and he must not be permitted to do so." Cheered by this news, the Yankees rallied and with tough fighting closed up their lines again.

On February 16 Confederate general Simon Bolivar Buckner understood the hopelessness of his plight. He sent a message through the lines to his old army friend, asking for favorable surrender terms. Quickly Grant responded with a note of his own. "No terms," it bluntly stated, "except an unconditional and immediate surrender can be accepted. I propose to move immediately upon your works." Caving in to Grant's demand, Buckner surrendered his entire army of close to 14,000 men.

"The news of the fall of Fort Donelson," Grant later remembered, "caused great delight all over the North." It was easily the greatest Union victory of the war so far. Everywhere people spoke proudly of U. S. Grant. "Unconditional Surrender" Grant they called him now. People excitedly read everything they could about their new hero. One newspaper story told of Grant calmly smoking a cigar in the midst of battle. Admiring citizens sent him hundreds of boxes of cigars. As a reward for his valor, Congress promoted Grant to major general.

During the next few weeks, Grant's army pushed south to clear the last of the enemy out of western Tennessee. In a desperate attempt to halt the Union advance, Confederate general Albert Sidney Johnston mounted a surprise attack. At Pittsburg Landing, Tennessee, charging rebel troops caught the Union army unprepared. Some critics later claimed Grant was off drinking when the fight began. Through the day of April 6, 1862, the Yankees clung to their positions in the dense woods around the Shiloh church. "It was a case of Southern dash against Northern pluck and endurance," Grant later exclaimed. Hour after hour the two armies grappled. Only darkness and a heavy rain ended the day's gory fighting.

Later General Sherman found his commander huddled beneath a tree in the rain. "Well, Grant," he remarked, "we've had the devil's own day, haven't we?"

"Yes," quietly answered Grant, puffing hard on his cigar. "Yes. Lick 'em tomorrow, though."

With the arrival of fresh troops, the stubborn Union general led a counterattack the next day. Now the rebel battle line wavered and cracked. The exhausted Confederates fled, dropping guns and knapsacks as they ran.

The Union army had won a victory but many Northerners gasped at the bloody cost. Even Grant admitted, "I saw an open field . . . so covered with dead that it would have been possible to walk across the clearing, in any direction, stepping on dead bodies, without a foot touching the ground." Some shocked politicians demanded Grant be relieved of duty. President Lincoln stood by his general, though. In order to win the war, he needed officers willing to fight.

As commander of the U.S. Army of Tennessee, by November 1862 Grant had gathered enough reinforcements to continue his march southward. A Confederate stronghold at the Mississippi River town of Vicksburg, Mississippi, presented an important goal. "So long as it was held by the enemy," Grant explained, "the free navigation of the river was prevented."

Through the next months Grant edged closer to Vicksburg's fortified river bluffs. Several times he showed his genius as he maneuvered for position and fought off Confederate attacks. If one effort failed, the stubborn general tried another. Union soldiers sunk to their hips as they struggled through bayous and swamps. In April 1863 Grant boldly cut his supply lines and crossed deep into enemy territory south and east of Vicksburg. For weeks the general's only personal baggage consisted of a toothbrush. Sleeping on the ground at night and living off the countryside by day, the encircling Union army finally laid siege to Vicksburg at the end of May.

The bitter siege of Vicksburg

Sweating soldiers dug rifle pits with picks and shovels. Others dragged artillery into position. Trapped inside Vicksburg, southern civilians and soldiers burrowed caves into the bluffs to escape the daily Union cannonfire. At last on July 3, 1863, Confederate general John Pemberton admitted defeat and surrendered his army of 30,000 men. On July 4 the beaten rebel soldiers marched out of Vicksburg and stacked their guns. Grant's stunning victory at Vicksburg (which occurred at the same time as the Union success at Gettysburg, Pennsylvania) struck a terrific blow against the South. Within days Union soldiers and sailors controlled all of the Mississippi River, cutting the Confederacy in two. Looking back over the Vicksburg campaign, President Lincoln happily declared that Grant's plan had been to "hold on with a bulldog grip and chew and choke as much as possible."

Confederate general Braxton Bragg

The War Department next called upon Grant to save the Union's Army of the Cumberland just then trapped in Chattanooga, Tennessee. Dazed at the horribly bloody battle of Chickamauga in Georgia, these troops had retreated into the little town of Chattanooga on the Tennessee River. Poised upon the heights surrounding the town from the south, General Braxton Bragg's Confederate troops confidently gazed down upon the penned-up Union army.

On October 22, 1863, Grant crossed the river into Chattanooga to take command of the besieged Union army. He discovered hungry Union soldiers standing listlessly about. Elsewhere horses, unfed for days, were dropping dead in the streets. "It looked, indeed," admitted Grant, "as if but two courses were open: one to starve, the other to surrender or be captured."

General Grant and some of his officers at Lookout Mountain

Sternly Grant refused to consider failure. He ordered that a rough mule trail be opened through the dense woods to the north. Union soldiers cheered as a steady supply of food and ammunition soon arrived in camp along this "cracker line." They now knew Grant intended to attack the enemy instead of waiting for defeat. On November 24 yelling Yankee troops charged up the rocky ledges of Lookout Mountain. By the end of the day the U.S. flag waved from the summit. The right side of the Union battle line was secure.

The next day Grant ordered attacks from the left and center. Seated on horseback he watched waves of Union troops gallantly charge across the open ground. Muskets

Union forces at the Battle of Chattanooga

cracked and gunsmoke rose in choking clouds as the
Yankees rushed ahead. At the foot of Missionary Ridge
they captured the Confederate rifle pits. Instead of stopping there, the troops excitedly continued up the slope.
"The fire along the rebel line was terrific," exclaimed
Grant. "The pursuit continued until the crest was reached
and soon our men were seen climbing over the Confederate barriers." Frantic rebel officers tried to keep their men
in position. A sudden panic gripped the rebels, though,
and thousands threw down their guns and ran. The charge
up Missionary Ridge had proven a complete triumph. Not
only had Grant saved Chattanooga, but by a miracle he had
routed the surrounding Confederate army.

# Chapter 6

# Hero of Appomattox

"With the aid of the noble armies that have fought in so many fields for our common country, it will be my earnest endeavor not to disappoint your expectations," Grant solemnly stated on March 9, 1864. Summoned to Washington, D.C., the hardened warrior accepted a commission as lieutenant general from President Lincoln, as well as command of all the Union armies in the field. Leaving his friend General Sherman in charge of the Union's western armies, Grant traveled to Virginia to supervise the actions of the North's Army of the Potomac. For two years these Yankee troops had been unable to destroy the Confederate Army of Northern Virginia commanded by General Robert E. Lee. Now Grant undertook the task to smash these rebels and capture the Confederate capital at Richmond.

Grant's grim strategy was to apply pressure on the enemy everywhere at once. While General Sherman's men battled the rebels in Georgia, Grant intended to grind away at Lee. For several weeks wagons rolled into camp carrying supplies and ammunition. Fresh recruits swelled Grant's army to 118,000 men.

Union troops advance against the Confederates in the Battle of the Wilderness.

"On to Richmond!" hurrahed the Union troops, as the spring 1864 campaign began. On May 4 the army crossed the Rapidan River and the next day encountered Lee's Confederates in a dense region called the Wilderness. For two days the Wilderness battle raged. Bloodied horses galloped wildly, cannonshells tore limbs from trees, and men fell screaming in pain. Fire broke out in the woods and many injured men burned to death. In the thick of the fight Grant sat whittling on sticks, calmly giving orders. Soon 17,000 Union troops lay killed or wounded. Still, Grant shifted his army to the south and tried to outflank Lee. At Spotsylvania Court House on May 12 the Yankees hammered at the Confederates again. "The enemy are fighting with great desperation," reported Grant. "We have lost many thousands of men killed and wounded and the enemy have no doubt lost more."

**The capture of a Confederate earthwork during the ten-month siege of Petersburg**

Unable to destroy Lee's army, Grant at least knew that he was wearing the rebels down. Stubbornly he vowed "to fight it out on this line if it takes all summer." Shifting south again he struck at the Confederates at Cold Harbor on June 3. In a gruesome frontal attack, 6,000 Union soldiers fell in less than an hour of fighting. The dreadful bloodshed shocked many Northerners. Some newspapers called Grant "The Butcher" and demanded he be replaced. Again President Lincoln insisted Grant was too valuable to lose. In the next weeks Grant's relentless pressure forced the Confederates to entrench along a forty-mile front. From the railroad center of Petersburg north to the Richmond capital, gray-clad Confederates faced battle-hardened federals across a barren no-man's-land.

The siege of Petersburg lasted ten months. While he waited for good weather, General Grant strengthened his army with fresh horses, equipment, and wagonloads of food. Every day Union cannons sent shells crashing into the Petersburg and Richmond streets, breaking the spirit of the rebels. In Georgia, General Sherman burned Atlanta and marched his army to the sea, destroying everything in his path. At the same time Union cavalry general Philip Sheridan advanced down Virginia's Shenandoah Valley, leaving burning barns and buildings behind him. "Give the enemy no rest," was Grant's standing order.

Right: Grant with generals Sherman (left) and Sheridan (right)

Below: The Battle of Atlanta, Georgia

Confederate general Robert E. Lee

The ruin of its factories and farms marked the doom of the Confederacy. Unable to supply his dwindling army, General Lee ordered a retreat on April 2, 1865. Gleeful Union troops raced into Petersburg and captured Richmond at last. Determined to crush Lee's army, Grant sent his troops dashing westward. The running battle lasted a week. April 9, 1865, found General Lee's exhausted force nearly surrounded near the village of Appomattox Court House, Virginia.

"There is nothing left [for] me to do but to go and see General Grant," concluded Lee, "and I would rather die a thousand deaths." Sadly he rode into the village to meet with Grant and surrender his army. At his headquarters Grant mounted his war-horse, Cincinnati, and trotted ahead. For four long years the tough general had waited for this day of final victory.

Grant entering the McLean house to receive Lee's surrender

At about one o'clock General Grant reached the southern edge of Appomattox Court House.

"Is Lee over there?" he quietly asked General Sheridan.

"Yes," answered Sheridan. "He's in that brick house."

"Well, then, we'll go over."

Grant climbed the steps of the two-story farmhouse owned by Wilmer McLean. Inside the parlor he greeted General Lee. Witnesses of the historic scene quickly noticed how different the two generals looked. Fifty-seven-year old General Robert E. Lee stood tall and gray, neatly dressed in the full uniform of his rank. "His manner and bearing were perfect," remarked newsman Sylvanus Cadwallader, "and stamped him a thoroughbred gentleman." Clearly General Lee represented the nobility of the Old South.

Grant and Lee meet to discuss the terms of surrender.

By contrast Ulysses S. Grant seemed to symbolize the simple, steadfast people of the North. Colonel Horace Porter remarked, "General Grant, then nearly forty-three years of age, was five foot eight inches in height, with shoulders slightly stooped. His hair and full beard were nut-brown, without a trace of gray in them. He had on his single-breasted blouse [coat] of dark-blue flannel . . . wore an ordinary pair of top-boots . . . and was without spurs. The boots and portions of his clothes were splattered with mud." Only the lieutenant general's stars sewn on his shoulders revealed Grant was anything more than a common private.

General Grant attempted to make pleasant conversation for a few minutes, until General Lee gently reminded him of the purpose of their meeting.

"I asked to see you," he said, "to ascertain upon what terms you would receive the surrender of my army."

"The terms I propose," the Union general answered firmly, "are those stated in my letter of yesterday — that is, the officers and men surrendered . . . and all arms, ammunition, and supplies to be delivered up as captured property."

Grant began writing out these surrender terms on paper. After gazing at General Lee's shining dress sword, he jotted the additional words: "This will not embrace the side arms of the officers, nor their private horses or baggage."

"This will have a very happy effect upon my army," remarked General Lee when he learned of Grant's generosity.

Then after a hesitant pause he asked, "The cavalrymen and artillerists own their own horses in our army. . . . I should like to understand whether these men will be permitted to retain their horses?"

Grant told him that according to the written terms they would not, until he saw Lee's saddened face.

"Well, the subject is quite new to me," the Union general quickly added, ". . . but I think this will be the last battle of the war. . . . I will arrange it this way. . . . I will instruct the officers . . . to let all the men who claim to own a horse or mule take the animals home with them to work their little farms."

While General Grant's secretary wrote formal copies of the surrender terms, Lee described the hungry condition of his army. "They have been living for the last few days upon parched corn." Promptly Grant ordered beef, bread, coffee, and sugar sent into the Confederate camp to feed the conquered enemy.

Just before four o'clock General Grant signed the surrender terms and General Lee presented his letter of acceptance. Lee shook hands with Grant, bowed to the other officers, and left the house. Soon after, General Grant strode across the McLean porch and started for his own headquarters. Riding toward his lines he heard Union cannon firing salutes at the glorious news of surrender. Immediately Grant ordered that this loud celebration be stopped. "The war is over," he kindly stated, "the rebels are our countrymen again." He saw no reason to shame the brave Southerners at the moment of their defeat.

Throughout the North, however, Americans soon openly rejoiced. In cities and towns church bells clanged, and on the rivers steamboat whistles shrieked. Through the streets citizens paraded waving flags, and in town squares they danced and yelled around blazing bonfires. Traveling to Washington, D.C., General Grant found himself mobbed by excited crowds wherever he went. His successes on the battlefield ranked him second only to Lincoln in reuniting the nation. Now the people wished to thank the man they proudly called "The Hero of Appomattox."

On April 14, 1865, General Grant attended a cabinet meeting at the White House. Grant expected the surrender of the last Confederate armies within days and spoke

President Abraham Lincoln, as photographed by Mathew Brady

hopefully of national peace. "Mrs. Grant was with me in Washington at the time," the general recalled, "and we were invited by President and Mrs. Lincoln to accompany them to the theatre on the evening of that day." Anxious to see his children, Grant turned down the invitation.

That night a crazed actor named John Wilkes Booth shot Lincoln at Ford's Theater. Grant hurried back to Washington, but the president died early the next day. "The joy that I had witnessed . . . when I left there had been turned to grief," commented Grant. "The city was in reality a city of mourning."

Citizens throughout the North bitterly blamed the South for Lincoln's murder. Angry Republican politicians vowed to avenge the ugly deed by punishing the southern states. Lincoln had hoped to forgive the South and smoothly reunite the nation. As new president Andrew Johnson tried to carry out Lincoln's policies, Grant continued his duties as commander in chief of the army.

During a visit with his parents he discovered his mother sewing. "Well, Ulysses," she calmly stated, hardly looking up from her needlework, "you've become a great man, haven't you?" Without a doubt the former leather goods clerk was now the most famous man in the country. In 1866 Congress promoted Grant to the newly-created rank of full general. The public showered him with praise and gifts, including a house in Galena, Illinois, and another in Philadelphia. That summer Grant accompanied President Johnson on a speaking tour across the North. During this "Swing Round the Circle," many crowds jeered President Johnson and his lenient policies toward the South. Everywhere, however, they greeted General Grant with wild cheers. "It looks . . . as if [General Grant is] to be the rising man," remarked Supreme Court Justice David Davis. "The people love military glory."

For a time Grant supported President Johnson, even serving as his temporary Secretary of War for five months in 1867. In 1868, however, the Radical Republicans who controlled Congress impeached President Johnson. They insisted he stand trial for blocking their attempts to punish the South. Johnson eventually was acquitted, but Grant did little to defend the president during this troubled time. By staying silent he improved his own chances of winning the Republican nomination for president that spring.

"I should like to be mayor of Galena [in order] to build a new sidewalk from my house to the depot," Grant had modestly said when people first mentioned him as a presidential candidate. Supporters, however, flattered him until he agreed to run. Grant was not a politician. He had

President Andrew Johnson

voted only once in his life. In spite of that, at the Republican national convention held in Chicago in May 1868, delegates excitedly chanted his name and nominated their hero on the first ballot. For vice-presidential candidate they picked Speaker of the House of Representatives Schuyler Colfax of Indiana. At their convention in New York City, Democrats chose New York governor Horatio Seymour to run against the general.

Throughout the summer and fall, Republicans and Democrats campaigned for their candidates. Seymour stumped across the nation promising fair treatment for the conquered South. At rallies, Democrats called Grant a drunkard and a military tyrant.

Grant's simple statement, "Let us have peace," became the slogan of the Republicans. The general spent most of the campaign quietly in Galena. In the meantime, Republican supporters worked hard in his behalf. In honor of Grant's early career as a leather worker, Tanner Clubs sprang up all over the country. Union veterans who favored Grant called themselves "The Boys in Blue" and marched in torchlight parades. At bonfires and barbecues Grant supporters cheered, "ONE! TWO! THREE! U! S! G! HURRAH!"

On election day, November 3, 1868, Americans walked to the polls to cast their votes. In the South black men, freed as a result of the war, proudly lined up to vote for the first time in a national election. Many white southern Democrats, however, were denied the right to vote because they had been Confederates. These two circumstances greatly helped the Republican party.

Through the night, telegraph wires hummed as they carried voting results to Galena. When the ballots were tallied they revealed the following counts:

|  | Popular Vote | Electoral Vote |
|---|---|---|
| Ulysses S. Grant | 3,013,650 | 214 |
| Horatio Seymour | 2,708,744 | 80 |

The people had elected the "Hero of Appomattox" eighteenth president of the United States.

Opposite page: The general who won the presidency

# Chapter 7

# Soldier in the White House

March 4, 1869, dawned with brisk, bright weather in Washington, D.C. Packed shoulder to shoulder on the grounds of the Capitol, a huge crowd eagerly awaited the inauguration ceremony. President Andrew Johnson bitterly refused to witness Grant take the oath of office. Unbothered, the mass of spectators watched with excitement as forty-seven-year-old Ulysses S. Grant stepped out onto the steps of the Capitol's east portico.

At 12:30, twenty-two cannons boomed a salute. Placing his hand on a Bible, Grant swore to "preserve and protect" the Constitution. Then he solemnly turned and read his inaugural speech. "The responsibilities of the position I feel, but accept them without fear," he declared. "The office has come to me unsought; I commence its duties untrammeled."

As president, Grant clearly meant well, but he soon showed his inexperience. To his cabinet and other important posts, he appointed many army friends as well as politicians who had done him personal favors. He trusted that these men would serve him with honest loyalty. Writer Henry Adams saw Grant's mistake and remarked, "A great soldier might be a baby politician."

Opposite page: A portrait of Grant
surrounded by scenes from his life

71

Nellie Grant with her father at his inauguration

Innocently President Grant also admired the nation's wealthiest, most powerful men. His new friendships with the rich soon caused him embarrassment. In the summer of 1869, stock investors Jay Gould and Jim Fisk set out to corner the nation's gold market. At fancy dinners and on yachting trips Gould and Fisk entertained the president. They tried to convince him not to sell any of the U.S. Treasury's gold supply on the stock exchange. In the meantime the two schemers kept buying gold, driving up the price. When Grant finally recognized the plot, he ordered four million dollars in federal gold to be sold. On Friday, September 24, 1869, gold prices abruptly fell. The immediate danger ended, but the "Black Friday" panic caused the ruin of many honest gold investors.

**Above: Stock investors James Fisk (left) and Jay Gould (right)**
**Below: Friends and office seekers crowd Grant's reception room.**

An 1870 cartoon showing the South suffering under the burden of carpetbagger rule during Reconstruction

The Radical Republicans in Congress also thought they could treat the president like a puppet. Since the Civil War, Congress had forced many disagreeable laws upon the southern states. President Grant accepted much of Congress's "Reconstruction" program. Many of its laws did help the freed slaves become full-fledged citizens.

Now divided into military districts, the conquered southern states were occupied by Union soldiers. Northern politicians carrying luggage fashioned from carpet material swarmed into the South to run the local governments. These "carpetbaggers" were often corrupt, openly buying the support of black voters and robbing state treasuries. Ex-Confederates bitterly sought ways to regain control of their states. Soon a secret organization called the

EXPERIENCE

## Among the Ku-Klux.

HARTFORD:
PUBLISHED BY THE AUTHOR.
1872.

A pamphlet describing
the cruelties of the
South's Ku Klux Klan

Ku Klux Klan rose up throughout the South. Disguised in ghostly robes and high peaked hoods, Klansmen nightly galloped across the countryside. Burning houses and brutally attacking enemies, they struck terror into the hearts of black voters and carpetbaggers alike.

In 1870 the states ratified the Fifteenth Amendment to the Constitution. This new law guaranteed all men in the United States the right to vote regardless of their "race, color, or previous condition of servitude." To further combat Ku Klux Klan tactics, President Grant signed several "force bills." These laws allowed the president to use military force to restore the peace. Soldiers could arrest anyone they wished for any reason. For a time the court system in the southern states lay in complete ruins.

The "wedding of the rails" at Promontory Point, Utah

In international affairs, President Grant failed to exercise much power. Throughout his four-year term he tried to buy the Caribbean island of Santo Domingo for the United States. Innocently Grant dreamed of sending the South's blacks there to live happily. When Congress turned aside this plan, Grant finally gave up the idea.

On the national scene, the end of the Civil War brought prosperity to the northern states. As people became richer, newspapers openly bragged that Americans were living in a "Gilded Age." Factory machinery thumped and whirred across the North, and whistles shrilly blew as railroad trains carried produce east and west. At Promontory Point in the Utah Territory, tracks of the Union Pacific Railroad and the Central Pacific Railroad finally met on May 10, 1869. Crowds cheered as the Golden Spike was driven into place, linking the United States from coast to coast.

As President Grant reached the end of his term, scandal rocked his administration. For years the Crédit Mobilier, a company connected with the Union Pacific Railroad, had been stealing profits during the building of the transcontinental railroad. Several important congressmen had profited from holding stock in the company. Vice-President Schuyler Colfax and other government officials were accused of taking bribes.

President Grant had no personal part in the Crédit Mobilier scandal. As the 1872 presidential campaign approached, he remained as popular as ever among most Republicans. At the Republican national convention in Philadelphia in June 1872, Grant received renomination for president on the first ballot. Delegates, however, dumped Vice-President Colfax and chose Massachusetts senator Henry Wilson to be Grant's running mate.

Liberal Republicans, angered about the weakness of Grant's administration, held a separate convention in Cincinnati. They nominated Horace Greeley to be their presidential candidate. The editor of the *New York Tribune*, Greeley once had advised ambitious young men to "Go West." Democrats supported Greeley, too.

During the 1872 presidential race, both candidates suffered ugly attacks. The *New York Sun* called the campaign "a shower of mud." Teased in cartoons and savagely insulted in newspaper stories, Greeley finally complained, "I have been assailed so bitterly that I hardly knew whether I was running for the Presidency or the penitentiary." Greeley campaigners in turn accused Grant of dishonesty, drunkenness, and stupidity.

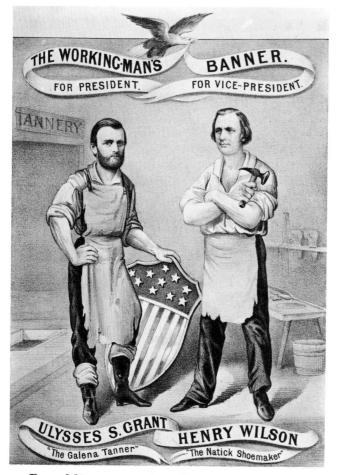

Campaign banner
for the 1872
Grant-Wilson
campaign

Republican speech makers reminded listeners of Grant's war record. Henry Wilson had been a successful shoemaker before entering politics. "The Tanner and the Cobbler!" yelled people who supported the Grant-Wilson ticket. As northern businessmen, Union war veterans, and blacks rallied behind Grant, it looked as though he would win an easy victory.

At the White House on November 5, 1872, the president puffed on his cigars and awaited the election day verdict. Soon newspaper headlines blared the voting results:

|  | Popular Vote | Electoral Vote |
|---|---|---|
| Ulysses S. Grant | 3,598,235 | 286 |
| Horace Greeley | 2,834,761 | 0 |

By an overwhelming margin, Grant had won a second term as president. His health completely broken by the hard campaign, on November 29, 1872, Horace Greeley died before all the electoral votes were tallied. Those votes Greeley did receive were not officially counted.

"I have been the subject of abuse and slander scarcely ever equalled in political history," complained President Grant in his second inaugural address on March 4, 1873. But government swindles during Grant's second term continued to blacken his administration.

Federal law required liquor distillers to pay taxes on the whiskey they made. Secret bribes to government officials allowed many distillers to sell untaxed alcohol. By 1875 the government had been cheated of millions of dollars by the "Whiskey Ring." When the fraud was uncovered, President Grant angrily insisted, "Let no guilty man escape." During the trials that followed, 110 conspirators were found guilty. President Grant, however, refused to believe that his own personal secretary, Orville Babcock, had accepted a bribe. With Grant's support, Babcock avoided conviction.

Other government workers took advantage of Grant's trust as well. Corrupt post office officials sold jobs and the Navy Department padded its payrolls. The crooked activities of the War Department shocked Congress in 1876. Evidence showed that Secretary of War William W. Belknap was taking bribes from traders at western Indian posts. These traders then sold shoddy goods to the Indians at high prices. To avoid punishment Secretary Belknap resigned his office in shame.

A Sioux Indian who survived the Battle of Little Big Horn (left); General Custer (right)

President Grant tried throughout his presidency to treat the Indians fairly. He named his friend Ely S. Parker, a Seneca Indian, as commissioner of Indian Affairs. Forced onto reservations and cruelly cheated by Indian agents and traders, though, many western Indians struck back. During Grant's years as president, Indians fought U.S. soldiers and settlers in over two hundred pitched battles. On June 25, 1876, a cavalry detachment commanded by General George Custer came upon a huge war party of Sioux Indians at the Little Big Horn River in Montana. In the bloody massacre that followed, some 1,500 Sioux warriors led by Chief Crazy Horse killed Custer and over 225 of his men. News of "Custer's Last Stand," the greatest victory in Indian warfare, shocked the entire nation.

Turmoil among Indians and settlers in the West and whites and blacks in the South lasted throughout the 1870s. The country needed strong leadership, but President Grant failed to provide it. The tough battlefield general simply placed too much faith in other people to do the work. As Grant's second term neared its end the country did experience some triumphs. Colorado joined the United States in 1876, adding the thirty-eighth proud star to the American flag. In Philadelphia excited citizens packed the Centennial Exposition. Tremendous growth in commerce and industry marked the United States' one-hundredth year as a nation.

Grant did not run for a third term in 1876. Instead the Republicans nominated Ohio governor Rutherford B. Hayes to run against New York's Democratic governor, Samuel Tilden. The 1876 presidential election proved so close that a special committee had to meet to make the final choice. Grant was pleased when Hayes finally was declared president. The general clearly recognized his own failure as the nation's leader. The many cases of government corruption had stained his White House years. "It was my fortune, or misfortune," he explained in his last annual message to Congress, "to be called to the office of Chief Executive without any previous political training. . . . Mistakes have been made, as all can see and I admit." Disappointed with his record, he later revealed, "I never wanted to get out of a place as much as I did to get out of the Presidency."

# Chapter 8

# The General's Last Fight

Its sails snapped in the breeze as the steamship *Indiana* cut through the Atlantic waves. Six weeks after leaving the White House, Grant, his wife, and his son Jesse set off on a world tour on May 17, 1877. Aristocrats and political leaders throughout Europe excitedly awaited a chance to meet the great American general. Huge crowds of common people also gathered everywhere Grant visited, hoping for a glimpse of the man who had "saved the Union."

The Grants first stopped in England. One night they slept at Windsor Castle and met Queen Victoria. During the summer they traveled through much of continental Europe. In the fall the Grants boarded a U.S. Navy ship and cruised the Mediterranean Sea. Stopping in Egypt, they explored the Nile River and gazed upon the pyramids. After visiting the ancient sites of the Holy Land and Turkey, they sailed to Italy and saw the classic cities of Florence, Venice, and Rome. In Spain, France, Norway, Belgium, and Russia, the Grants received honored treatment everywhere they went.

**Opposite page: Grant in retirement at Mount McGregor**

Having crisscrossed most of Europe and the Mediterranean, the hardy travelers chose next to visit Asia. In India they walked through the tranquil gardens of the Taj Mahal and in Siam the king entertained them at his court. Masses of curious people lined the Grants' route through China. The Japanese received them with even greater interest and respect. In a formal ceremony Grant visited the Imperial Palace. Breaking national tradition, the emperor stepped forward and shook the general's hand.

"I am both homesick and dread going home," Grant remarked as his long world tour neared its end. In the fall of 1879 the travelers sailed across the Pacific to California. During the next months Grant explored the American West as well as Cuba and Mexico. When Republicans spoke of running him for president again in 1880 he encouraged the idea. At the national convention he led the voting for a number of ballots before finally losing the nomination to Ohio congressman James Garfield.

In need of income, the Grants moved to New York City in 1881. With his savings of $100,000, Grant entered into a partnership with Wall Street businessman Ferdinand Ward. The brokerage firm of Grant and Ward attracted thousands of investors. Unhappily, Ward proved to be a scoundrel who bought stocks carelessly and juggled the ledgers to hide his mistakes. In May 1884 the firm suddenly sank into bankruptcy. Overnight Ward's swindles left Grant completely penniless. "I have made it a rule of my life to trust a man long after other people gave him up," the general gloomily remarked, "but I don't see how I can ever trust any human being again."

**Above: Grant with Chinese
Grand Secretary of State
Li Hung Chang in 1879**

**Right: A cartoon showing
Grant leaving office after
two terms as president**

In the midst of his financial troubles, Grant suffered an even worse misfortune. One day while eating a peach, he felt a sharp pain at the base of his tongue. A doctor's examination revealed that he had cancer. Years of heavy cigar smoking finally had taken their toll.

Grant received this terrible news with silent courage. As the disease progressed, his only thought was to save his wife and family from poverty before he died. Grant had written several articles for *Century Magazine* describing his recollections of Shiloh, Vicksburg, and other battles. These stories proved so popular that several book publishers had asked Grant to write a book. Samuel Clemens (better known by his pen name, Mark Twain) was the successful author of *The Adventures of Tom Sawyer*. As a partner in the publishing firm of Charles L. Webster & Company, Clemens offered a handsome contract if Grant would write his memoirs.

With determination Grant accepted the assignment. Through the summer and fall he dictated his memoirs until his throat grew too sore and hoarse. Thereafter, sitting with a writing pad on his lap he scribbled page after page of his personal history himself. All the nation knew Grant was racing against death to finish his work. Coughing spells and days of horrible pain slowed his progress, but still he refused to give up.

In June of 1885 the Grant family became guests at a country home in Mount McGregor, New York. Curious visitors who passed the house sometimes saw the ex-president sitting on the porch bundled in blankets and shawls. As his body wasted away with cancer, he increased his

**Grant writing his memoirs at Mount McGregor**

writing efforts. "This is my great interest in life," he wrote to his son Fred, "to see my work done."

"These volumes are dedicated to the American soldier and sailor," began *The Personal Memoirs of U.S. Grant.* In crisp, direct language the book described his life and campaigns to the end of the Civil War. On July 16, 1885, Grant's shaky pencil made its last correction in the long text. Hugely successful, the book eventually would earn Julia Grant over $400,000.

"There is nothing more I should do to it now," scrawled Grant in pain when he was done, "and therefore I am not likely to be more ready to go than at this moment." His task completed, the sixty-three-year-old general surrendered to cancer at last. In the early morning hours of July 23, 1885, Grant's family remained at his bedside. His pulse faded and his breathing grew weaker. Asked if he wanted anything, he whispered, "Water," and a wet sponge was touched to his lips. At 8:00 A.M., Ulysses S. Grant died, knowing he had provided for his family.

It seemed all the nation mourned Grant's death. One million people packed the streets of New York City to watch the somber funeral procession. Thousands of others gathered along Riverside Drive in New York City in 1897 when President William McKinley dedicated Grant's impressive permanent tomb.

During his full life Ulysses S. Grant had known the heights of success and the depths of failure. Clearly it was his military career that marked him for his greatest fame. "I never went into a battle willingly or with enthusiasm," Grant once honestly stated. Yet he never turned away from a fight, and it was this fearlessness that made him such a hero. "I have carefully searched the military records of both ancient and modern history," his old enemy General Robert E. Lee once declared, "and have never found Grant's superior as a general."

"Let Us Have Peace" are the words engraved upon Grant's tomb. As Lincoln's most valued general, Ulysses S. Grant gave a precious gift to all Americans. He fought to save the Union and won lasting peace for the United States.

**Opposite page: Grant on his deathbed**

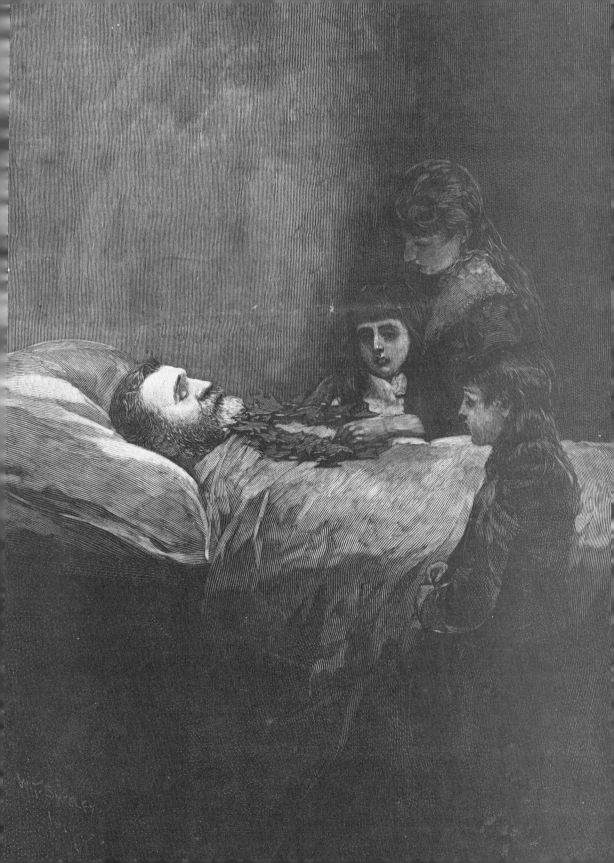

# Chronology of American History

(Shaded area covers events in Ulysses S. Grant's lifetime.)

**About A.D. 982**—Eric the Red, born in Norway, reaches Greenland in one of the first European voyages to North America.

**About 1000**—Leif Ericson (Eric the Red's son) leads what is thought to be the first European expedition to mainland North America; Leif probably lands in Canada.

**1492**—Christopher Columbus, seeking a sea route from Spain to the Far East, discovers the New World.

**1497**—John Cabot reaches Canada in the first English voyage to North America.

**1513**—Ponce de Léon explores Florida in search of the fabled Fountain of Youth.

**1519-1521**—Hernando Cortés of Spain conquers Mexico.

**1534**—French explorers led by Jacques Cartier enter the Gulf of St. Lawrence in Canada.

**1540**—Spanish explorer Francisco Coronado begins exploring the American Southwest, seeking the riches of the mythical Seven Cities of Cibola.

**1565**—St. Augustine, Florida, the first permanent European town in what is now the United States, is founded by the Spanish.

**1607**—Jamestown, Virginia, is founded, the first permanent English town in the present-day U.S.

**1608**—Frenchman Samuel de Champlain founds the village of Quebec, Canada.

**1609**—Henry Hudson explores the eastern coast of present-day U.S. for the Netherlands; the Dutch then claim parts of New York, New Jersey, Delaware, and Connecticut and name the area New Netherland.

**1619**—The English colonies' first shipment of black slaves arrives in Jamestown.

**1620**—English Pilgrims found Massachusetts' first permanent town at Plymouth.

**1621**—Massachusetts Pilgrims and Indians hold the famous first Thanksgiving feast in colonial America.

**1623**—Colonization of New Hampshire is begun by the English.

**1624**—Colonization of present-day New York State is begun by the Dutch at Fort Orange (Albany).

**1625**—The Dutch start building New Amsterdam (now New York City).

**1630**—The town of Boston, Massachusetts, is founded by the English Puritans.

**1633**—Colonization of Connecticut is begun by the English.

**1634**—Colonization of Maryland is begun by the English.

**1636**—Harvard, the colonies' first college, is founded in Massachusetts. Rhode Island colonization begins when Englishman Roger Williams founds Providence.

**1638**—Delaware colonization begins as Swedes build Fort Christina at present-day Wilmington.

**1640**—Stephen Daye of Cambridge, Massachusetts prints *The Bay Psalm Book*, the first English-language book published in what is now the U.S.

**1643**—Swedish settlers begin colonizing Pennsylvania.

**About 1650**—North Carolina is colonized by Virginia settlers.

**1660**—New Jersey colonization is begun by the Dutch at present-day Jersey City.

**1670**—South Carolina colonization is begun by the English near Charleston.

**1673**—Jacques Marquette and Louis Jolliet explore the upper Mississippi River for France.

**1682**—Philadelphia, Pennsylvania, is settled. La Salle explores Mississippi River all the way to its mouth in Louisiana and claims the whole Mississippi Valley for France.

**1693**—College of William and Mary is founded in Williamsburg, Virginia.

**1700**—Colonial population is about 250,000.

**1703**—Benjamin Franklin is born in Boston.

**1732**—George Washington, first president of the U.S., is born in Westmoreland County, Virginia.

**1733**—James Oglethorpe founds Savannah, Georgia; Georgia is established as the thirteenth colony.

**1735**—John Adams, second president of the U.S., is born in Braintree, Massachusetts.

**1737**—William Byrd founds Richmond, Virginia.

**1738**—British troops are sent to Georgia over border dispute with Spain.

**1739**—Black insurrection takes place in South Carolina.

**1740**—English Parliament passes act allowing naturalization of immigrants to American colonies after seven-year residence.

**1743**—Thomas Jefferson is born in Albemarle County, Virginia. Benjamin Franklin retires at age thirty-seven to devote himself to scientific inquiries and public service.

**1744**—King George's War begins; France joins war effort against England.

**1745**—During King George's War, France raids settlements in Maine and New York.

**1747**—Classes begin at Princeton College in New Jersey.

**1748**—The Treaty of Aix-la-Chapelle concludes King George's War.

**1749**—Parliament legally recognizes slavery in colonies and the inauguration of the plantation system in the South. George Washington becomes the surveyor for Culpepper County in Virginia.

**1750**—Thomas Walker passes through and names Cumberland Gap on his way toward Kentucky region. Colonial population is about 1,200,000.

**1751**—James Madison, fourth president of the U.S., is born in Port Conway, Virginia. English Parliament passes Currency Act, banning New England colonies from issuing paper money. George Washington travels to Barbados.

**1752**—Pennsylvania Hospital, the first general hospital in the colonies, is founded in Philadelphia. Benjamin Franklin uses a kite in a thunderstorm to demonstrate that lightning is a form of electricity.

**1753**—George Washington delivers command that the French withdraw from the Ohio River Valley; French disregard the demand. Colonial population is about 1,328,000.

**1754**—French and Indian War begins (extends to Europe as the Seven Years' War). Washington surrenders at Fort Necessity.

**1755**—French and Indians ambush Braddock. Washington becomes commander of Virginia troops.

**1756**—England declares war on France.

**1758**—James Monroe, fifth president of the U.S., is born in Westmoreland County, Virginia.

**1759**—Cherokee Indian war begins in southern colonies; hostilities extend to 1761. George Washington marries Martha Dandridge Custis.

**1760**—George III becomes king of England. Colonial population is about 1,600,000.

**1762**—England declares war on Spain.

**1763**—Treaty of Paris concludes the French and Indian War and the Seven Years' War. England gains Canada and most other French lands east of the Mississippi River.

**1764**—British pass the Sugar Act to gain tax money from the colonists. The issue of taxation without representation is first introduced in Boston. John Adams marries Abigail Smith.

**1765**—Stamp Act goes into effect in the colonies. Business virtually stops as almost all colonists refuse to use the stamps.

**1766**—British repeal the Stamp Act.

**1767**—John Quincy Adams, sixth president of the U.S. and son of second president John Adams, is born in Braintree, Massachusetts. Andrew Jackson, seventh president of the U.S., is born in Waxhaw settlement, South Carolina.

**1769**—Daniel Boone sights the Kentucky Territory.

**1770**—In the Boston Massacre, British soldiers kill five colonists and injure six. Townshend Acts are repealed, thus eliminating all duties on imports to the colonies except tea.

**1771**—Benjamin Franklin begins his autobiography, a work that he will never complete. The North Carolina assembly passes the "Bloody Act," which makes rioters guilty of treason.

**1772**—Samuel Adams rouses colonists to consider British threats to self-government.

**1773**—English Parliament passes the Tea Act. Colonists dressed as Mohawk Indians board British tea ships and toss 342 casks of tea into the water in what becomes known as the Boston Tea Party. William Henry Harrison is born in Charles City County, Virginia.

**1774**—British close the port of Boston to punish the city for the Boston Tea Party. First Continental Congress convenes in Philadelphia.

**1775**—American Revolution begins with battles of Lexington and Concord, Massachusetts. Second Continental Congress opens in Philadelphia. George Washington becomes commander-in-chief of the Continental army.

**1776**—Declaration of Independence is adopted on July 4.

**1777**—Congress adopts the American flag with thirteen stars and thirteen stripes. John Adams is sent to France to negotiate peace treaty.

**1778**—France declares war against Great Britain and becomes U.S. ally.

**1779**—British surrender to Americans at Vincennes. Thomas Jefferson is elected governor of Virginia. James Madison is elected to the Continental Congress.

**1780**—Benedict Arnold, first American traitor, defects to the British.

**1781**—Articles of Confederation go into effect. Cornwallis surrenders to George Washington at Yorktown, ending the American Revolution.

**1782**—American commissioners, including John Adams, sign peace treaty with British in Paris. Thomas Jefferson's wife, Martha, dies. Martin Van Buren is born in Kinderhook, New York.

**1784**—Zachary Taylor is born near Barboursville, Virginia.

**1785**—Congress adopts the dollar as the unit of currency. John Adams is made minister to Great Britain. Thomas Jefferson is appointed minister to France.

**1786**—Shays's Rebellion begins in Massachusetts.

**1787**—Constitutional Convention assembles in Philadelphia, with George Washington presiding; U.S. Constitution is adopted. Delaware, New Jersey, and Pennsylvania become states.

**1788**—Virginia, South Carolina, New York, Connecticut, New Hampshire, Maryland, and Massachusetts become states. U.S. Constitution is ratified. New York City is declared U.S. capital.

**1789**—Presidential electors elect George Washington and John Adams as first president and vice-president. Thomas Jefferson is appointed secretary of state. North Carolina becomes a state. French Revolution begins.

**1790**—Supreme Court meets for the first time. Rhode Island becomes a state. First national census in the U.S. counts 3,929,214 persons. John Tyler is born in Charles City County, Virginia.

**1791**—Vermont enters the Union. U.S. Bill of Rights, the first ten amendments to the Constitution, goes into effect. District of Columbia is established. James Buchanan is born in Stony Batter, Pennsylvania.

**1792**—Thomas Paine publishes *The Rights of Man*. Kentucky becomes a state. Two political parties are formed in the U.S., Federalist and Republican. Washington is elected to a second term, with Adams as vice-president.

**1793**—War between France and Britain begins; U.S. declares neutrality. Eli Whitney invents the cotton gin; cotton production and slave labor increase in the South.

**1794**—Eleventh Amendment to the Constitution is passed, limiting federal courts' power. "Whiskey Rebellion" in Pennsylvania protests federal whiskey tax. James Madison marries Dolley Payne Todd.

**1795**—George Washington signs the Jay Treaty with Great Britain. Treaty of San Lorenzo, between U.S. and Spain, settles Florida boundary and gives U.S. right to navigate the Mississippi. James Polk is born near Pineville, North Carolina.

**1796**—Tennessee enters the Union. Washington gives his Farewell Address, refusing a third presidential term. John Adams is elected president and Thomas Jefferson vice-president.

**1797**—Adams recommends defense measures against possible war with France. Napoleon Bonaparte and his army march against Austrians in Italy. U.S. population is about 4,900,000.

**1798**—Washington is named commander-in-chief of the U.S. Army. Department of the Navy is created. Alien and Sedition Acts are passed. Napoleon's troops invade Egypt and Switzerland.

**1799**—George Washington dies at Mount Vernon, New York. James Monroe is elected governor of Virginia. French Revolution ends. Napoleon becomes ruler of France.

**1800**—Thomas Jefferson and Aaron Burr tie for president. U.S. capital is moved from Philadelphia to Washington, D.C. The White House is built as presidents' home. Spain returns Louisiana to France. Millard Fillmore is born in Locke, New York.

**1801**—After thirty-six ballots, House of Representatives elects Thomas Jefferson president, making Burr vice-president. James Madison is named secretary of state.

**1802**—Congress abolishes excise taxes. U.S. Military Academy is founded at West Point, New York.

**1803**—Ohio enters the Union. Louisiana Purchase treaty is signed with France, greatly expanding U.S. territory.

**1804**—Twelfth Amendment to the Constitution rules that president and vice-president be elected separately. Alexander Hamilton is killed by Vice-President Aaron Burr in a duel. Orleans Territory is established. Napoleon crowns himself emperor of France. Franklin Pierce is born in Hillsborough Lower Village, New Hampshire.

**1805**—Thomas Jefferson begins his second term as president. Lewis and Clark expedition reaches the Pacific Ocean.

**1806**—Coinage of silver dollars is stopped; resumes in 1836.

**1807**—Aaron Burr is acquitted in treason trial. Embargo Act closes U.S. ports to trade.

**1808**—James Madison is elected president. Congress outlaws importing slaves from Africa. Andrew Johnson is born in Raleigh, North Carolina.

**1809**—Abraham Lincoln is born near Hodgenville, Kentucky.

**1810**—U.S. population is 7,240,000.

**1811**—William Henry Harrison defeats Indians at Tippecanoe. Monroe is named secretary of state.

**1812**—Louisiana becomes a state. U.S. declares war on Britain (War of 1812). James Madison is reelected president. Napoleon invades Russia.

**1813**—British forces take Fort Niagara and Buffalo, New York.

**1814**—Francis Scott Key writes "The Star-Spangled Banner." British troops burn much of Washington, D.C., including the White House. Treaty of Ghent ends War of 1812. James Monroe becomes secretary of war.

**1815**—Napoleon meets his final defeat at Battle of Waterloo.

**1816**—James Monroe is elected president. Indiana becomes a state.

**1817**—Mississippi becomes a state. Construction on Erie Canal begins.

**1818**—Illinois enters the Union. The present thirteen-stripe flag is adopted. Border between U.S. and Canada is agreed upon.

**1819**—Alabama becomes a state. U.S. purchases Florida from Spain. Thomas Jefferson establishes the University of Virginia.

**1820**—James Monroe is reelected. In the Missouri Compromise, Maine enters the Union as a free (non-slave) state.

1821—Missouri enters the Union as a slave state. Santa Fe Trail opens the American Southwest. Mexico declares independence from Spain. Napoleon Bonaparte dies.

1822—U.S. recognizes Mexico and Colombia. Liberia in Africa is founded as a home for freed slaves. Ulysses S. Grant is born in Point Pleasant, Ohio. Rutherford B. Hayes is born in Delaware, Ohio.

1823—Monroe Doctrine closes North and South America to European colonizing or invasion.

1824—House of Representatives elects John Quincy Adams president when none of the four candidates wins a majority in national election. Mexico becomes a republic.

1825—Erie Canal is opened. U.S. population is 11,300,000.

1826—Thomas Jefferson and John Adams both die on July 4, the fiftieth anniversary of the Declaration of Independence.

1828—Andrew Jackson is elected president. Tariff of Abominations is passed, cutting imports.

1829—James Madison attends Virginia's constitutional convention. Slavery is abolished in Mexico. Chester A. Arthur is born in Fairfield, Vermont.

1830—Indian Removal Act to resettle Indians west of the Mississippi is approved.

1831—James Monroe dies in New York City. James A. Garfield is born in Orange, Ohio. Cyrus McCormick develops his reaper.

1832—Andrew Jackson, nominated by the new Democratic Party, is reelected president.

1833—Britain abolishes slavery in its colonies. Benjamin Harrison is born in North Bend, Ohio.

1835—Federal government becomes debt-free for the first time.

1836—Martin Van Buren becomes president. Texas wins independence from Mexico. Arkansas joins the Union. James Madison dies at Montpelier, Virginia.

1837—Michigan enters the Union. U.S. population is 15,900,000. Grover Cleveland is born in Caldwell, New Jersey.

1840—William Henry Harrison is elected president.

1841—President Harrison dies in Washington, D.C., one month after inauguration. Vice-President John Tyler succeeds him.

1843—William McKinley is born in Niles, Ohio.

1844—James Knox Polk is elected president. Samuel Morse sends first telegraphic message.

1845—Texas and Florida become states. Potato famine in Ireland causes massive emigration from Ireland to U.S. Andrew Jackson dies near Nashville, Tennessee.

1846—Iowa enters the Union. War with Mexico begins.

1847—U.S. captures Mexico City.

1848—John Quincy Adams dies in Washington, D.C. Zachary Taylor becomes president. Treaty of Guadalupe Hidalgo ends Mexico-U.S. war. Wisconsin becomes a state.

1849—James Polk dies in Nashville, Tennessee.

1850—President Taylor dies in Washington, D.C.; Vice-President Millard Fillmore succeeds him. California enters the Union, breaking tie between slave and free states.

1852—Franklin Pierce is elected president.

1853—Gadsden Purchase transfers Mexican territory to U.S.

1854—"War for Bleeding Kansas" is fought between slave and free states.

1855—Czar Nicholas I of Russia dies, succeeded by Alexander II.

1856—James Buchanan is elected president. In Massacre of Potawatomi Creek, Kansas-slavers are murdered by free-staters. Woodrow Wilson is born in Staunton, Virginia.

1857—William Howard Taft is born in Cincinnati, Ohio.

1858—Minnesota enters the Union. Theodore Roosevelt is born in New York City.

1859—Oregon becomes a state.

**1860**—Abraham Lincoln is elected president; South Carolina secedes from the Union in protest.

**1861**—Arkansas, Tennessee, North Carolina, and Virginia secede. Kansas enters the Union as a free state. Civil War begins.

**1862**—Union forces capture Fort Henry, Roanoke Island, Fort Donelson, Jacksonville, and New Orleans; Union armies are defeated at the battles of Bull Run and Fredericksburg. Martin Van Buren dies in Kinderhook, New York. John Tyler dies near Charles City, Virginia.

**1863**—Lincoln issues Emancipation Proclamation: all slaves held in rebelling territories are declared free. West Virginia becomes a state.

**1864**—Abraham Lincoln is reelected. Nevada becomes a state.

**1865**—Lincoln is assassinated in Washington, D.C., and succeeded by Andrew Johnson. U.S. Civil War ends on May 26. Thirteenth Amendment abolishes slavery. Warren G. Harding is born in Blooming Grove, Ohio.

**1867**—Nebraska becomes a state. U.S. buys Alaska from Russia for $7,200,000. Reconstruction Acts are passed.

**1868**—President Johnson is impeached for violating Tenure of Office Act, but is acquitted by Senate. Ulysses S. Grant is elected president. Fourteenth Amendment prohibits voting discrimination. James Buchanan dies in Lancaster, Pennsylvania.

**1869**—Franklin Pierce dies in Concord, New Hampshire.

**1870**—Fifteenth Amendment gives blacks the right to vote.

**1872**—Grant is reelected over Horace Greeley. General Amnesty Act pardons ex-Confederates. Calvin Coolidge is born in Plymouth Notch, Vermont.

**1874**—Millard Fillmore dies in Buffalo, New York. Herbert Hoover is born in West Branch, Iowa.

**1875**—Andrew Johnson dies in Carter's Station, Tennessee.

**1876**—Colorado enters the Union. "Custer's last stand": he and his men are massacred by Sioux Indians at Little Big Horn, Montana.

**1877**—Rutherford B. Hayes is elected president as all disputed votes are awarded to him.

**1880**—James A. Garfield is elected president.

**1881**—President Garfield is assassinated and dies in Elberon, New Jersey. Vice-President Chester A. Arthur succeeds him.

**1882**—U.S. bans Chinese immigration. Franklin D. Roosevelt is born in Hyde Park, New York.

**1884**—Grover Cleveland is elected president. Harry S. Truman is born in Lamar, Missouri.

**1885**—Ulysses S. Grant dies in Mount McGregor, New York.

**1886**—Statue of Liberty is dedicated. Chester A. Arthur dies in New York City.

**1888**—Benjamin Harrison is elected president.

**1889**—North Dakota, South Dakota, Washington, and Montana become states.

**1890**—Dwight D. Eisenhower is born in Denison, Texas. Idaho and Wyoming become states.

**1892**—Grover Cleveland is elected president.

**1893**—Rutherford B. Hayes dies in Fremont, Ohio.

**1896**—William McKinley is elected president. Utah becomes a state.

**1898**—U.S. declares war on Spain over Cuba.

**1900**—McKinley is reelected. Boxer Rebellion against foreigners in China begins.

**1901**—McKinley is assassinated by anarchist Leon Czolgosz in Buffalo, New York; Theodore Roosevelt becomes president. Benjamin Harrison dies in Indianapolis, Indiana.

**1902**—U.S. acquires perpetual control over Panama Canal.

**1903**—Alaskan frontier is settled.

**1904**—Russian-Japanese War breaks out. Theodore Roosevelt wins presidential election.

1905—Treaty of Portsmouth signed, ending Russian-Japanese War.

1906—U.S. troops occupy Cuba.

1907—President Roosevelt bars all Japanese immigration. Oklahoma enters the Union.

1908—William Howard Taft becomes president. Grover Cleveland dies in Princeton, New Jersey. Lyndon B. Johnson is born near Stonewall, Texas.

1909—NAACP is founded under W.E.B. DuBois

1910—China abolishes slavery.

1911—Chinese Revolution begins. Ronald Reagan is born in Tampico, Illinois.

1912—Woodrow Wilson is elected president. Arizona and New Mexico become states.

1913—Federal income tax is introduced in U.S. through the Sixteenth Amendment. Richard Nixon is born in Yorba Linda, California. Gerald Ford is born in Omaha, Nebraska.

1914—World War I begins.

1915—British liner *Lusitania* is sunk by German submarine.

1916—Wilson is reelected president.

1917—U.S. breaks diplomatic relations with Germany. Czar Nicholas of Russia abdicates as revolution begins. U.S. declares war on Austria-Hungary. John F. Kennedy is born in Brookline, Massachusetts.

1918—Wilson proclaims "Fourteen Points" as war aims. On November 11, armistice is signed between Allies and Germany.

1919—Eighteenth Amendment prohibits sale and manufacture of intoxicating liquors. Wilson presides over first League of Nations; wins Nobel Peace Prize. Theodore Roosevelt dies in Oyster Bay, New York.

1920—Nineteenth Amendment (women's suffrage) is passed. Warren Harding is elected president.

1921—Adolf Hitler's stormtroopers begin to terrorize political opponents.

1922—Irish Free State is established. Soviet states form USSR. Benito Mussolini forms Fascist government in Italy.

1923—President Harding dies in San Francisco, California; he is succeeded by Vice-President Calvin Coolidge.

1924—Coolidge is elected president. Woodrow Wilson dies in Washington, D.C. James Carter is born in Plains, Georgia. George Bush is born in Milton, Massachusetts.

1925—Hitler reorganizes Nazi Party and publishes first volume of *Mein Kampf.*

1926—Fascist youth organizations founded in Germany and Italy. Republic of Lebanon proclaimed.

1927—Stalin becomes Soviet dictator. Economic conference in Geneva attended by fifty-two nations.

1928—Herbert Hoover is elected president. U.S. and many other nations sign Kellogg-Briand pacts to outlaw war.

1929—Stock prices in New York crash on "Black Thursday"; the Great Depression begins.

1930—Bank of U.S. and its many branches close (most significant bank failure of the year). William Howard Taft dies in Washington, D.C.

1931—Emigration from U.S. exceeds immigration for first time as Depression deepens.

1932—Franklin D. Roosevelt wins presidential election in a Democratic landslide.

1933—First concentration camps are erected in Germany. U.S. recognizes USSR and resumes trade. Twenty-First Amendment repeals prohibition. Calvin Coolidge dies in Northampton, Massachusetts.

1934—Severe dust storms hit Plains states. President Roosevelt passes U.S. Social Security Act.

1936—Roosevelt is reelected. Spanish Civil War begins. Hitler and Mussolini form Rome-Berlin Axis.

1937—Roosevelt signs Neutrality Act.

1938—Roosevelt sends appeal to Hitler and Mussolini to settle European problems amicably.

1939—Germany takes over Czechoslovakia and invades Poland, starting World War II.

**1940**—Roosevelt is reelected for a third term.

**1941**—Japan bombs Pearl Harbor, U.S. declares war on Japan. Germany and Italy declare war on U.S.; U.S. then declares war on them.

**1942**—Allies agree not to make separate peace treaties with the enemies. U.S. government transfers more than 100,000 Nisei (Japanese-Americans) from west coast to inland concentration camps.

**1943**—Allied bombings of Germany begin.

**1944**—Roosevelt is reelected for a fourth term. Allied forces invade Normandy on D-Day.

**1945**—President Franklin D. Roosevelt dies in Warm Springs, Georgia; Vice-President Harry S. Truman succeeds him. Mussolini is killed; Hitler commits suicide. Germany surrenders. U.S. drops atomic bomb on Hiroshima; Japan surrenders; end of World War II.

**1946**—U.N. General Assembly holds its first session in London. Peace conference of twenty-one nations is held in Paris.

**1947**—Peace treaties are signed in Paris. "Cold War" is in full swing.

**1948**—U.S. passes Marshall Plan Act, providing $17 billion in aid for Europe. U.S. recognizes new nation of Israel. India and Pakistan become free of British rule. Truman is elected president.

**1949**—Republic of Eire is proclaimed in Dublin. Russia blocks land route access from Western Germany to Berlin; airlift begins. U.S., France, and Britain agree to merge their zones of occupation in West Germany. Apartheid program begins in South Africa.

**1950**—Riots in Johannesburg, South Africa, against apartheid. North Korea invades South Korea. U.N. forces land in South Korea and recapture Seoul.

**1951**—Twenty-Second Amendment limits president to two terms.

**1952**—Dwight D. Eisenhower resigns as supreme commander in Europe and is elected president.

**1953**—Stalin dies; struggle for power in Russia follows. Rosenbergs are executed for espionage.

**1954**—U.S. and Japan sign mutual defense agreement.

**1955**—Blacks in Montgomery, Alabama, boycott segregated bus lines.

**1956**—Eisenhower is reelected president. Soviet troops march into Hungary.

**1957**—U.S. agrees to withdraw ground forces from Japan. Russia launches first satellite, *Sputnik*.

**1958**—European Common Market comes into being. Fidel Castro begins war against Batista government in Cuba.

**1959**—Alaska becomes the forty-ninth state. Hawaii becomes fiftieth state. Castro becomes premier of Cuba. De Gaulle is proclaimed president of the Fifth Republic of France.

**1960**—Historic debates between Senator John F. Kennedy and Vice-President Richard Nixon are televised. Kennedy is elected president. Brezhnev becomes president of USSR.

**1961**—Berlin Wall is constructed. Kennedy and Khrushchev confer in Vienna. In Bay of Pigs incident, Cubans trained by CIA attempt to overthrow Castro.

**1962**—U.S. military council is established in South Vietnam.

**1963**—Riots and beatings by police and whites mark civil rights demonstrations in Birmingham, Alabama; 30,000 troops are called out, Martin Luther King, Jr., is arrested. Freedom marchers descend on Washington, D.C., to demonstrate. President Kennedy is assassinated in Dallas, Texas; Vice-President Lyndon B. Johnson is sworn in as president.

**1964**—U.S. aircraft bomb North Vietnam. Johnson is elected president. Herbert Hoover dies in New York City.

**1965**—U.S. combat troops arrive in South Vietnam.

**1966**—Thousands protest U.S. policy in Vietnam. National Guard quells race riots in Chicago.

**1967**—Six-Day War between Israel and Arab nations.

**1968**—Martin Luther King, Jr., is assassinated in Memphis, Tennessee. Senator Robert Kennedy is assassinated in Los Angeles. Riots and police brutality take place at Democratic National Convention in Chicago. Richard Nixon is elected president. Czechoslovakia is invaded by Soviet troops.

**1969**—Dwight D. Eisenhower dies in Washington, D.C. Hundreds of thousands of people in several U.S. cities demonstrate against Vietnam War.

**1970**—Four Vietnam War protesters are killed by National Guardsmen at Kent State University in Ohio.

**1971**—Twenty-Sixth Amendment allows eighteen-year-olds to vote.

**1972**—Nixon visits Communist China; is reelected president in near-record landslide. Watergate affair begins when five men are arrested in the Watergate hotel complex in Washington, D.C. Nixon announces resignations of aides Haldeman, Ehrlichman, and Dean and Attorney General Kleindienst as a result of Watergate-related charges. Harry S. Truman dies in Kansas City, Missouri.

**1973**—Vice-President Spiro Agnew resigns; Gerald Ford is named vice-president. Vietnam peace treaty is formally approved after nineteen months of negotiations. Lyndon B. Johnson dies in San Antonio, Texas.

**1974**—As a result of Watergate cover-up, impeachment is considered; Nixon resigns and Ford becomes president. Ford pardons Nixon and grants limited amnesty to Vietnam War draft evaders and military deserters.

**1975**—U.S. civilians are evacuated from Saigon, South Vietnam, as Communist forces complete takeover of South Vietnam.

**1976**—U.S. celebrates its Bicentennial. James Earl Carter becomes president.

**1977**—Carter pardons most Vietnam draft evaders, numbering some 10,000.

**1980**—Ronald Reagan is elected president.

**1981**—President Reagan is shot in the chest in assassination attempt. Sandra Day O'Connor is appointed first woman justice of the Supreme Court.

**1983**—U.S. troops invade island of Grenada.

**1984**—Reagan is reelected president. Democratic candidate Walter Mondale's running mate, Geraldine Ferraro, is the first woman selected for vice-president by a major U.S. political party.

**1985**—Soviet Communist Party secretary Konstantin Chernenko dies; Mikhail Gorbachev succeeds him. U.S. and Soviet officials discuss arms control in Geneva. Reagan and Gorbachev hold summit conference in Geneva. Racial tensions accelerate in South Africa.

**1986**—Space shuttle *Challenger* explodes shortly after takeoff; crew of seven dies. U.S. bombs bases in Libya. Corazon Aquino defeats Ferdinand Marcos in Philippine presidential election.

**1987**—Iraqi missile rips the U.S. frigate *Stark* in the Persian Gulf, killing thirty-seven American sailors. Congress holds hearings to investigate sale of U.S. arms to Iran to finance Nicaraguan *contra* movement.

**1988**—President Reagan and Soviet leader Gorbachev sign INF treaty, eliminating intermediate nuclear forces. Severe drought sweeps the United States. George Bush is elected president.

**1989**—East Germany opens Berlin Wall, allowing citizens free exit. Communists lose control of governments in Poland, Romania, and Czechoslovakia. Chinese troops massacre over 1,000 pro-democracy student demonstrators in Beijing's Tiananmen Square.

**1990**—Iraq annexes Kuwait, provoking the threat of war. East and West Germany are reunited. The Cold War between the United States and the Soviet Union comes to a close. Several Soviet republics make moves toward independence.

**1991**—Backed by a coalition of members of the United Nations, U.S. troops drive Iraqis from Kuwait. Latvia, Lithuania, and Estonia withdraw from the USSR. The Soviet Union dissolves as its republics secede to form a Commonwealth of Independent States.

**1992**—U.N. forces fail to stop fighting in territories of former Yugoslavia. More than fifty people are killed and more than six hundred buildings burned in rioting in Los Angeles. U.S. unemployment reaches eight-year high. Hurricane Andrew devastates southern Florida and parts of Louisiana. International relief supplies and troops are sent to combat famine and violence in Somalia.

**1993**—U.S.-led forces use airplanes and missiles to attack military targets in Iraq. William Jefferson Clinton becomes the forty-second U.S. president.

**1994**—Richard M. Nixon dies in New York City.

# Index

Page numbers in boldface type indicate illustrations.

## About the Author

Zachary Kent grew up in Little Falls, New Jersey, and received an English degree from St. Lawrence University. Following college he worked at a New York City literary agency for two years and then launched his writing career. To support himself while writing, he has worked as a taxi driver, a shipping clerk, and a house painter. Mr. Kent has had a lifelong interest in American history. Studying the U.S. presidents was his childhood hobby. His collection of presidential items includes books, pictures, and games, as well as several autographed letters.